Original title:
You'll Come Back to Yourself

Copyright © 2024 Book Fairy Publishing
All rights reserved.

Editor: Theodor Taimla
Author: Melani Helimets
ISBN HARDBACK: 978-9916-756-84-3
ISBN PAPERBACK: 978-9916-756-85-0

Epiphany of Silence

In the midst of clamor, silence breathes,
A whispered truth in endless seas,
Where stillness gives the mind release,
And restless hearts find peace with ease.

A gift unseen, its presence loud,
Silence wears an unseen shroud,
Beckoning dreams from behind a cloud,
In quietude, we're unbowed.

Thoughts like waves in silent tide,
In tranquil depths, no need to hide,
The soul's true voice, there beside,
In silence, wisdom does reside.

Embrace the calm, the hush, the pause,
Silence speaks without a cause,
Revealing truths in silent laws,
In stillness, find life's grand applause.

A moment's breath, a silent plea,
In quiet, find clarity,
Epiphany in silence, free,
The heart's pure path, its decree.

The Forgotten Song

In shadows cast by time's embrace,
A melody lost, without a trace,
It lingers softly, whispers low,
A tune that only echoes know.

Once vibrant chords, now faded grey,
In silent halls, where memories play,
The notes dissolve in twilight's light,
A spectral dance, beyond our sight.

Though centuries may come and pass,
The song endures in mourning grass,
A lullaby for hearts once strong,
Now beating to the forgotten song.

Echoes of Serenity

In tranquil waters, dreams are born,
With whispers of the early morn,
A breeze that carries peace so rare,
A touch of calm upon the air.

Mountains stand as ancient guards,
Seas reflect in tranquil shards,
The earth beneath, a stable friend,
With every curve, it seems to mend.

Time slows down in valley's green,
A silent world, serene, unseen,
Echoes drift through mist and trees,
An ode to everlasting ease.

The Quiet Awakening

Morning dew on virgin fields,
As life unfolds, its secrets yields,
Soft whispers of a waking day,
In dawn's embrace, we gently sway.

Each moment new, a breath of grace,
A journey starts at nature's pace,
With every step, a silent vow,
To cherish all, the why and how.

Sunrise paints the skies in gold,
A story ancient, yet retold,
In quiet dawn, the world reclaims,
The birth of hope, in tender flames.

Through Inner Doors

In silent rooms, where thoughts reside,
Behind the eyes, where feelings hide,
A labyrinth of dreams and fears,
Through inner doors, beyond the years.

Each corridor a path to tread,
With echoes of what once was said,
In chambers deep, where truths unfold,
Stories of the heart are told.

Mysteries in shadows cast,
By memories, from first to last,
Through every door, a life reveals,
The tender depths, the soul conceals.

Fragments Rejoined

In the mosaic of our days,
Lost pieces seek their place.
Echoes from forgotten ways,
Find shelter in your grace.

Splinters shape a hidden whole,
Mended by time's gentle hand.
Whispers of a fractured soul,
Rediscover where they stand.

Broken shards of memory,
Weave into a seamless thread.
Craft a tale of harmony,
From fragments we have shed.

Found in Reflection

Mirror calm reflects our fears,
Shadows dance in quiet night.
Inward gaze reveals our tears,
Contours drawn by morning light.

Deep within the silent glass,
Echoes of a life once known.
Fleeting moments come to pass,
Leave their marks on hearts alone.

Journeys from the past replay,
Paths we never thought to tread.
Found in quiet light of day,
Truths we once so gently fled.

Silent Rediscovery

Muted tones of twilight fall,
Whisper secrets to the winds.
Echoes through the shadowed hall,
Speak of where the quiet ends.

In the hush of falling night,
Hidden dreams begin to bloom.
Whispers guiding, out of sight,
Lead away from silent gloom.

Reborn in the softest sigh,
Hidden truths begin to claim.
Voices past that didn't die,
Whisper soft, and call our name.

Soul's Reawakening

Embers glow in midnight dark,
Calling out to sleeping hearts.
Promise of a morning spark,
Bids the shadows to depart.

Awakened by the dawn's warm touch,
Dreams once lost become anew.
Soul remembers, yearns as such,
To the light it bids adieu.

Rising from that quiet deep,
Breath anew from silent spring.
Soul's reawakening from sleep,
Finds a voice, begins to sing.

Echoes of Home

Softly through the leafy glade,
Whispers of the past invade,
Memories by moonlight's glow,
Echoes of a place we know.

Footsteps on a weathered floor,
Opening that creaking door,
A fragrance in the autumn air,
Home is found within a prayer.

The laughter dancing through the trees,
A melody upon the breeze,
Hearts entwined in endless grace,
Home is more than just a place.

Resonance of Self

In the stillness of the mind,
Truths we often seek to find,
Reflections ripple, deep and clear,
In the quiet, we draw near.

A journey through the soul's own stream,
Awakens from a distant dream,
Whispers of a hidden tale,
Within the self, a setting sail.

In echoes of our silent thoughts,
Wisdom's voice is never lost,
Resonance of self takes flight,
Guided by an inner light.

The Heart's Compass

Beneath the starry, boundless sky,
A compass guides where dreams can fly,
True north found within desire,
Leads us through the darkest mire.

Hope like whispers, soft and brave,
Calls from love's eternal wave,
The heart's true course, it charts unseen,
In every shade of life between.

Trust in paths that lie ahead,
Feel the pulse where fears have fled,
The heart's compass, strong and bright,
Steers us through the endless night.

Unveiling the Inner Light

Hidden 'neath the surface, deep,
Lies a light we always keep,
In the shadows, it may hide,
Yet it glows from deep inside.

Journey through the veils of doubt,
Find the flame that won't burn out,
With each step, we come to see,
We are more than we believe.

Light of courage, light of grace,
Shining from a sacred place,
Unveil the light, so pure and bright,
Guiding us through darkest night.

Heart's Hearth

In the quiet of the night,
Where whispers softly tread,
There burns a gentle light,
A hearth where dreams are bred.

With embers glowing bright,
It warms the heart anew,
A beacon in the night,
Guiding me to you.

Through the storm's assault,
And winter's icy breath,
It holds without a fault,
A warmth that conquers death.

Here within this space,
Where love's pure light is found,
We find our sacred place,
On shared and hallowed ground.

So let the fire glow,
In the sanctuary's depth,
With every breath we sow,
The heart's eternal cleft.

Back to the Bedrock

Down where the roots extend,
Deep into earth's embrace,
Foundations never bend,
They hold a timeless grace.

Through layers of the past,
Unyielding and unshaken,
They stand through ages vast,
A legacy unbroken.

In strife and in repose,
They anchor firm and true,
As granite's heartfelt prose,
They whisper what we knew.

Connecting sky to soil,
Impassioned and enduring,
Through centuries they toil,
In quiet strength assuring.

Return to where we started,
To bedrock deep and ancient,
With hearts forever guarded,
In earth's eternal cadence.

Reawakening the Source

From slumber deep and dark,
Where shadows thickly linger,
A spark becomes a mark,
And ignites with just a finger.

A river deep within,
Begins its course anew,
With each resounding din,
Its waters break on through.

Revived from dormant streams,
Flows forth with mighty force,
Awakening old dreams,
Reviving dormant course.

The pulse begins to quicken,
As life renews its path,
The air is charged and thickened,
With nature's vital wrath.

From source to destination,
It travels far and wide,
A journey's transformation,
Rediscovered, undenied.

Rediscovering Shadows

In corners dim and dappled,
Where light and darkness blend,
There secrets remain grappled,
In shadows that descend.

Each shade a whispered story,
Of what has been concealed,
A dance of faded glory,
In shadows now revealed.

The silent, patient cast,
Of memories in gray,
Which time had thought to last,
Yet slowly melts away.

Rediscovered lines,
Drawn in the dusky pen,
Of histories and signs,
Forgotten until then.

So with a careful eye,
We seek what lies beneath,
The shadows tell no lie,
In twilight's truthful sheath.

Of Shadows and Light

In twilight's soft embrace,
Where shadows dance and play,
The night begins its chase,
Of light that gently sways.

A whisper in the dark,
The secrets shadows hold,
Their stories leave a mark,
In whispers often bold.

Light shimmers, it reveals,
The hidden and the known,
Through shadows, it appeals,
To hearts that feel alone.

Together they entwine,
A dance of dark and bright,
In harmony, they sign,
The song of day and night.

So let the shadows be,
And let the light emerge,
For in their dance we see,
The beauty they converge.

The Gentle Reclaim

A touch of tender grace,
By nature's gentle hand,
It claims its own sweet space,
In every part of land.

The wind whispers through trees,
The soothing sounds of peace,
It carries autumn's leaves,
In dances that won't cease.

Mountains stand tall and wise,
With secrets ages old,
They watch the endless skies,
And nature's wonders mold.

Oceans with waves that roam,
Soft tides that ebb and flow,
They find their journey home,
In rhythms we all know.

Nature's gentle reclaim,
A love that knows no bound,
It heals, it mends, no shame,
In silence so profound.

Roots and Branches

Beneath the forest's green,
Where roots run deep and true,
The earth's own quiet scene,
With stories it imbues.

Branches reaching high,
To skies of endless blue,
Their whispers as they sigh,
A timeless tale ensues.

Leaves that dance and sway,
In breezes soft and light,
They bring a joyful play,
To mornings clear and bright.

Roots that ground and hold,
The secrets of the past,
Through years both young and old,
Their strength forever lasts.

So listen to the trees,
Their wisdom in each ring,
In roots and branches, see,
The songs they'll always sing.

Embers of Truth

In the hearth of yesteryears,
Where stories come to rest,
The embers of our fears,
In silence have confessed.

A flicker of a flame,
The truths we dare not speak,
Yet in the fire's name,
Their warmth is what we seek.

Through shadows they do rise,
The echoes of our past,
In embers we surmise,
The lessons meant to last.

Each spark a chosen thought,
Of wisdom forged in time,
In fires we have wrought,
A balance so divine.

So let the embers glow,
With truths both old and new,
For in their gentle show,
Our hearts will find what's true.

Returning to the Core

In the stillness of the night,
Where shadows softly sway,
I return to my own light,
In the calmest of the day.

Layers of my being peel,
Revealing what is true,
In the depths, I begin to feel,
The essence born anew.

Awake within this silent roar,
As echoes touch the soul,
Returning to the heart's core,
Where love and life console.

Each breath a gentle guide,
Each moment pure and clear,
In simplicity I reside,
Away from doubt and fear.

Grounded in this sacred place,
Where inner lights ignite,
I find a gentle, timeless grace,
A beacon shining bright.

Familiar Echoes

Whispers on the evening breeze,
Voices from the past,
Familiar echoes through the trees,
In memories, I'm cast.

Faces fade but feelings stay,
Like shadows at twilight,
In the heart, they find a way,
To guide me through the night.

Songs once sung and stories told,
Resonate once more,
In echoes I can still behold,
What time cannot restore.

In the silence I can hear,
Each laugh and every tear,
Echoes of a love sincere,
That always lingers near.

Though the days may swiftly part,
Their spirits always show,
For familiar beats of heart,
In echoes gently flow.

Rediscovered Paths

Winding roads and ancient trails,
Through forests deep and dark,
Rediscovering the tales,
Of life's enduring mark.

Paths once walked but long forgot,
Now come into the light,
Each step forward, every thought,
A journey to the night.

Finding ways through tangled vines,
To places once unknown,
In the quest, the heart aligns,
To times that it has shown.

Rediscovered, not by chance,
But through a soul's demand,
Walking through life's timeless dance,
Guided by the hand.

Trails of wonder, paths of old,
Reveal what time has spun,
As stories ancient now unfold,
Beneath a setting sun.

The Inner Journey

A voyage not of land or sea,
But through the self within,
Where truth and awareness be,
And self-discovery begins.

Through valleys of the mind I go,
Through peaks of hope and fear,
An inner light begins to show,
A path that's ever clear.

In chambers of the deepest heart,
Where echoes of dreams reside,
I find the courage to depart,
And let my spirit guide.

Bound not by time or by space,
This journey into me,
Reveals in every quiet place,
A glimpse of what can be.

With every step and gentle breath,
To wisdom's core I steer,
On paths that lead beyond death,
To joy forever near.

The Timeless Self

Within the mirror's soft embrace,
A visage both old and new,
Timeless seals the fleeting face,
In memories blurred, yet true.

Shadows of yesteryears appear,
And whisper tales they've spun,
In silent voices, calm and clear,
Of battles lost and won.

A journey marked by every scar,
Through deserts wide and cold,
To mountaintops where dreams afar,
In golden light unfold.

Each wrinkle tells a story proud,
Of laughter, love, and strife,
In the ticking clock that shouts aloud,
The saga of a life.

The mirror now a crystal sphere,
Reflecting heart and mind,
In it, the timeless self is near,
Eternal and intertwined.

Awaken to the Echo

Morning's light through windows break,
A whisper stirs the dawn,
As echoes from the dreams we make,
Call softly and are gone.

In the hush of waking thought,
A memory unfolds,
Of lessons life and love have taught,
In stories yet untold.

The echoes of a distant song,
Retrieve a distant past,
Awakening where we belong,
In moments made to last.

Each note a gem of precious thread,
Woven in our sleep,
Awake, to follow where we're led,
To secrets that we keep.

In every breath, the echoes sway,
A dance of time's own rhyme,
Awake, embrace the newfound day,
With rhythms of the sublime.

Return to the Hive

In fields where golden nectar lies,
The worker bees do hum,
A melody that splits the skies,
A song where all are one.

Through flowers bright, the journey goes,
With wings that never tire,
Back to the hive, where sweetness flows,
And hearts with joy aspire.

The hive a temple built on trust,
On unity's pure thread,
In every bee, a common thrust,
In every hue, deep red.

Together in the hive we find,
A sanctuary blessed,
A labyrinth where paths entwined,
Lead weary souls to rest.

So fly dear heart, where love is born,
And every dream survives,
In fields of honey, greet the morn,
Return to sacred hives.

Rejoining the Tapestry

Lives woven in a silent thread,
A tapestry of days,
Where every tear and joy is spread,
In myriad, endless ways.

Through fibers of the heart so vast,
Our stories intertwine,
Each pattern shapes a future past,
In colors bold, divine.

Rejoining where the needle goes,
To stitch the soul's embrace,
In gentle turns, the fabric grows,
A testament to grace.

Seasons mark the flowing strands,
With nature's vibrant hues,
And time slips through our open hands,
In daydreams we peruse.

At last the tapestry complete,
Its beauty plain to see,
We find our place, in lines so sweet,
Rejoined eternally.

Reclaiming the Inner Light

Through the clouds, a beam strikes true,
Awakening dreams from night.
Within the shadows, courage grew,
To reclaim the inner light.

Waves of doubt crash on shores,
Yet within, the fire roars.
Heartbeats echo ancient lore,
Guiding through forgotten doors.

In stillness, soft whispers arise,
Embers flicker and ignite.
With each breath, hope defies,
Embracing dawn after night.

Paths untread reveal their grace,
Courage finds a sacred pace.
Inward journeys interlace,
Souls renewed, fears effaced.

Now amidst the quiet bloom,
Burdens shed, the sky turns bright.
From the heart's transcendent womb,
Reclaimed, the inner light.

Echoes Within

Echoes linger in the mind,
Soft as whispers, strong as love.
In the halls where dreams unwind,
Seeking stars in skies above.

Memories, both dark and bright,
Resonate through time and space.
In the silent, endless night,
Find connection, find the trace.

Songs of yore, with harmony,
Weave through sinews of the soul.
Threads of past, a legacy,
Hope in fragments, makes us whole.

Whispers of the winds unseen,
Murmur stories left untold.
In the spaces in-between,
Truths discovered, hearts consoled.

From the depths where echoes play,
Rise the voices, soft and thin.
In their echoes, night and day,
Finding strength, echoes within.

Harmony Restored

In chaos, we sought the calm,
In tumult, the peace was found.
Under stars, a soothing balm,
Harmony restored, profound.

Nature's symphony conspired,
To remind us of our place.
In the balance long desired,
Found our rhythm, found our grace.

Through the tempest, through the storm,
Unified, our spirits free.
In the dance, the perfect form,
Echoes through eternity.

Hearts aligned, and minds attuned,
In the midst of life's grand song.
Harmony, a sacred rune,
Where all souls have long belonged.

In the silences between,
Listen, sense the love implored.
In each breath, the space serene,
Lives were healed, harmony restored.

Ancestral Whispers

Ancient voices call my name,
From the earth and from the sky.
In the breath of wind, they came,
Guiding me, though paths awry.

Stories etched in blood and bone,
Echo through the canyons deep.
Legacy, the seeds well-sown,
In the silence as we sleep.

Wisdom passed through shadowed halls,
Whispers where the spirits dwell.
Ancestral voices tear down walls,
In their truths, our hearts they swell.

From the ashes, rise anew,
Phoenix flames of courage stirred.
With each step, my soul they drew,
Closer to the ancient word.

In the twilight, hear the song,
Echoes that forever roam.
Ancestral whispers, ever strong,
Calling me, calling me home.

Threads of Identity

Woven tapestry of dreams,
Interlacing fears and hopes.
In each thread, a hidden meme,
Within fabric's vast scopes.

Patterns tell of battles old,
Mirrored in the warp and weft.
Every strand has stories bold,
In the keepsakes we have kept.

Colors blend in harmony,
Crafting who we are today.
Embrace our diversity,
In the woven bright display.

We stitch tales of ancestry,
Generations intertwined.
In each loop, our legacy,
By our hands, our hearts defined.

Woven threads of identity,
Binding together as one.
In this fabric, unity,
Our collective self begun.

Resurgence of Self

In the shadows of the night,
Where the echoes softly fall.
Find the strength to claim the light,
Answering the inner call.

Lost within the thickest haze,
Fragments of a used-to-be.
Striving through the darkest maze,
Seeking hope's benign decree.

Rise from cinders, fierce and bright,
Renaissance from deep within.
Dusting off the cloak of night,
Casting shadows to the wind.

With each breath, a spark ignites,
Fueling fires ever brave.
Burning through the longest nights,
Through the tempest, spirits save.

Resurgence of the self, we find,
Reborn in the blazing light.
Crafting futures intertwined,
Emerging strong from endless night.

Rekindling the Flame

In the quiet of the dawn,
Sparks of passion reappear.
From the ashes mostly gone,
A new fervor casts its cheer.

Embers smolder in the dark,
Waiting for a breath to claim.
Gentle winds ignite the spark,
Kindling once a dormant flame.

Deep within the heart, it lies,
Silent yet alive and strong.
Patient for the time to rise,
In its aura, dreams prolong.

Each small blaze, a guiding light,
Through the trials we must face.
Warming hearts within its sight,
Granting solace and embrace.

Rekindling the flame, we find,
Purpose gleams in every ray.
In its warmth, we'll intertwine,
Building hope anew each day.

Essence Restored

In the garden of the mind,
Where the soul's tenacity,
Bound by vines once intertwined,
Withers crushed complexity.

Silent whispers of the breeze,
Bringing tales of days gone by.
Amidst the rustling of the trees,
Echoes of our spirits' cry.

From the depths, a bloom appears,
Unfolding with each sunrise.
Washing off our buried fears,
In its beauty, we arise.

Tides of healing, smooth and slow,
Erode the walls that bind the heart.
Sense of self begins to grow,
In every recreated part.

Essence restored, our sights align,
Paths unveiled before our eyes.
In our core, stars brightly shine,
Emanating through the skies.

Deep Within

In shadows quiet, hearts do beat,
Within the depths, no light does meet.
Where whispers soft, in echoes ring,
The soul's true voice begins to sing.

Amidst the dark, a spark ignites,
A flicker grows, in warming nights.
From hidden wells of silent cries,
A dawning trust within does rise.

Reflections dance on mirrors deep,
As secrets long in silence sleep.
They stir awake, with tender care,
Revealing truths that linger there.

Embrace the night where depths reside,
For in its grasp, we cannot hide.
With courage found in shadows thin,
We journey inward, deep within.

The Circle Completes

In cycles vast, life's woven thread,
Through time's embrace, we're gently led.
From dawn to dusk, the moments blend,
In circle's path, there is no end.

Beyond the sky, beneath the ground,
A rhythm constant, e'er profound.
As seasons shift and tides retreat,
The circle's dance is truly sweet.

From birth to death, we trace the line,
A journey marked by the divine.
Each step we take, each breath we meet,
The circle forms, our lives complete.

In joy and pain, we find our place,
Within the circle's warm embrace.
Through every turn, we come to see,
The endless loop of eternity.

Embodied Familiarity

In every touch, a memory's spark,
A gentle kiss upon the dark.
In eyes that meet, familiar grace,
We find our home, a sacred place.

The echoes of a thousand dreams,
Surface in the silent streams.
As bodies move in perfect time,
Their rhythms form a seamless rhyme.

Each heartbeat knows, within its core,
The paths we've walked, the wounds we've bore.
Through every scar and joyous fling,
Our spirits rise and softly sing.

In warm embrace, we recognize,
The kindred soul, the mirrored ties.
In every breath, a sweet decree,
Embodied delicately.

Navigating the Soul

Through vast expanse of inner sea,
We sail on waves of mystery.
In quiet depths, our compass guides,
To hidden shores our soul abides.

The wind it whispers ancient tales,
That stir the heart like ocean gales.
With each enlightened thought we gain,
We navigate through joy and pain.

Stars above and dreams below,
Illuminate the path we go.
By moonlight soft and sunbeam bright,
We find our truth in darkest night.

Chart the course with loving hand,
Through waters deep, where spirits stand.
On journey long, by heart made whole,
We navigate the boundless soul.

Embrace the Void

In shadows deep, I find my peace,
Where silence reigns, time seems to cease,
The stars above in dark array,
Guide my soul, they light the way.

The void, a canvas vast and wide,
Holds secrets of the universe inside,
A whisper here, a cosmic song,
In it's embrace, I feel I belong.

No fears consume, no worries bind,
In endless night, my heart aligned,
A dance of particles and light,
With the void, everything feels right.

Fragments Reunited

Pieces scattered, torn apart,
Fragments of a broken heart,
Yet in the dust, a shimmer finds,
A mosaic formed through patient minds.

A shard of hope, a glint of care,
Threads of dreams interlaced there,
Each piece a story, each chip a tale,
Together strong, we shall prevail.

In unity, the fragments blend,
Creating patterns that transcend,
A masterpiece, through trials wrought,
Reunited, from chaos caught.

Echoes of the Heart

In quiet nights, the heart does speak,
Echoes of dreams, both bold and meek,
A melody of love and loss,
Reflecting on the paths we've crossed.

The pulse of life in whispered tones,
Resonates in silent zones,
Each beat a memory, clear and deep,
In the echoes, our secrets keep.

The heart, a drum, vibrant and strong,
Beating forth its timeless song,
Through echoes, it forever finds,
A rhythm true, in fleeting times.

Silent Awakening

In dawn's light, the silence breaks,
A whisper in the soul awakes,
The world in stillness, softly hums,
A new day's promise gently comes.

The flowers bloom, in quiet grace,
The morning sun, a warm embrace,
In silence, wisdom's voice is clear,
Guiding steps as shadows clear.

Awakened now, the mind takes flight,
To realms where dreams merge with light,
Through silent paths, our spirits soar,
To find the truths worth yearning for.

Journey to the Core

Beneath the earth, where secrets lie,
Ancient roots and shadows sigh.
Through molten rivers, fearless we glide,
Seeking the flame, where dreams reside.

Each layer peeled, a tale unfolds,
In whispers soft, the past remolds.
To the core, with heart and mind,
Truths of old we seek to find.

Stone and fire, a dance so grand,
Elements forged by nature's hand.
In the depth, where silence screams,
We uncover hidden dreams.

Bound by courage, we descend,
To the world's very end.
The heart of earth we dare explore,
On this journey to the core.

Whispers of the Soul

In the quiet of the night,
When the stars are shining bright,
There are whispers soft and low,
From the places we don't know.

Gentle breezes carry tales,
From the mountains to the vales.
Each soul whispers its own song,
Of the place where it belongs.

Through the darkness, through the light,
In the morning, in the night,
Listen close, and you will hear,
Whispers from a world so near.

Silent voices, lost in time,
Echo in a subtle rhyme.
In each whisper, there's a goal,
To find the beauty of the soul.

Beyond the Veil

Beyond the veil, where shadows dance,
Lies a realm of sweet romance.
Mysteries deep, yet to unfold,
Stories timeless, tales untold.

Shimmering light, in twilight's glow,
Secrets hidden, start to show.
Through the mist, we step inside,
Where realities collide.

Questions linger, answers hide,
In this world, where dreams reside.
Eyes wide open, hearts entwined,
Truths beyond what minds can find.

Journey through the midnight shade,
With courage, the path is made.
Beyond the veil, we find our place,
In the vast and boundless space.

Through Time's Lens

Through time's lens, we take a glance,
At moments past, in timeless dance.
Images clear, yet far away,
Echoes of another day.

History's touch on every scene,
Futures glimpsed with visions keen.
Layers of time, a rich expanse,
Unfolding tales at every chance.

Generations weave their thread,
Voices of the past now shed,
In the tapestry of years,
Laughter, sorrow, hopes, and fears.

Through the lens, the future's nigh,
Guided by the ancient sigh,
Time's embrace, a gentle blend,
Where beginnings meet the end.

From Ashes Reborn

In the silence of dawn, whispers of change,
A phoenix rises, new and strange.
The embers glow, the shadows mourn,
In every end, a life reborn.

From ruins high, to sky's embrace,
A soul finds light in darkest space.
Through trials fierce and fires sworn,
Emerges bright, from ashes reborn.

Each feather scorched, each heartbeat sings,
Of ancient fires and new beginnings.
The night gives way, the day adorns,
This tale of life, from ashes reborn.

With wings of flame and a heart of steel,
A journey new begins to heal.
In every dawn, the truth is worn,
In every heart, from ashes reborn.

So rise anew, with courage found,
Leave behind the ashen ground.
For in each soul, a beacon born,
A shining light, from ashes reborn.

The Silent Garden

Beneath the boughs where shadows play,
In whispered winds, the flowers sway.
A tranquil realm, where time stands still,
The silent garden, nature's will.

The dew-kissed leaves, in morning's grace,
Reflect the calm of nature's face.
No sound disturbs, no discord mars,
In silent gardens, 'neath the stars.

Each petal holds a tale untold,
Of whispered dreams and hearts of gold.
In quietude, where peace is worn,
The silent garden, quietly born.

Beneath the moon, the lilies gleam,
In softest light, a gentle dream.
A world untouched by human plight,
In silent gardens, pure delight.

Here solace finds a heart so true,
In every leaf and sky so blue.
A sacred place where souls align,
The silent garden, so divine.

Inner Constellations

In the night, the stars align,
Mapping dreams through space and time.
Each glimmer like a heart's elation,
Guiding us, our constellations.

Beyond the sky, within our minds,
A universe of thoughts unwinds.
Galaxies of pure creation,
Our boundless inner constellations.

Through cosmic thoughts and stardust hues,
Our spirits sail where light ensues.
A dance of endless fascination,
Amongst the inner constellations.

With every breath, a nebulae,
Of hopes and fears that intertwine.
A milky way of pure foundation,
Built from inner constellations.

So gaze within where stars ignite,
A universe in endless flight.
Through every night and day's rotation,
Shine our inner constellations.

Melody of the Core

Deep within, where silence reigns,
A melody begins its strains.
A heartbeat pure, a tune so sure,
The haunting song of the soul's core.

In every breath, in every sigh,
A note is born, it floats on high.
Uniting worlds through sepulchred door,
The endless melody of the core.

In darkness deep, it weaves a light,
A symphony of gleaming night.
Through heartache fierce and joy's encore,
This melody at our very core.

Each pulse a rhythm, life's true song,
Echoes vast where we belong.
In quiet tones or myriad roar,
We hear the melody of the core.

So listen close with patient ear,
The music's voice, so strong and clear.
Within us all, forever more,
Resides the melody of the core.

Within the Silence

In quiet chambers of the mind,
Where shadows dance, but none unkind,
A whisper grows with soft amen,
And peace descends from deep within.

The stars converse with night's embrace,
A solace found in empty space,
Beneath the moon's reflective glow,
In silence, secrets start to show.

Unspoken words on gentle breeze,
In stillness, hearts begin to ease,
The world's noise fades, a distant hum,
Within the silence, truth will come.

Here dreams are woven, breath by breath,
In lullaby of life and death,
Each heartbeat's pause, a sacred art,
In quietude, we find our heart.

The echoes of a soul's release,
Where silence brings a sound of peace,
A symphony, in whispers fair,
Within the silence, we are there.

Metamorphosis of the Heart

An ember glows amidst the dark,
A tiny spark ignites the bark,
Through trials faced and battles won,
A transformation has begun.

From chrysalis to skyward flight,
The heart unfolds in morning light,
With every beat, a story told,
Of calloused past to spirit bold.

In shadows past, it sought retreat,
But now it marches, dancing feet,
A melody of love's sweet claim,
The heart reborn, without the shame.

The metamorphosis of pain,
To learn to laugh and love again,
A journey brave, through tempests wild,
Emerges now a freer child.

Wings unfurled, it soars above,
With newfound strength and boundless love,
The heart has blossomed, pure and free,
In metamorphosis, the key.

Hidden Horizons

Beyond the edge of sight we gaze,
Where dreams converge and spirits raise,
A hidden world, unseen by day,
Invites us forth to find our way.

In night's embrace, horizons call,
A whispered promise to us all,
To seek the treasures, seldom known,
In shadows cast by twilight's tone.

Each step we take on paths unknown,
Reveals a truth, a seed that's sown,
For in the hidden, lies the spark,
That guides us through the vast and dark.

Mountains rise and valleys dip,
In distant lands our senses sip,
A taste of wonder, pure and bright,
In hidden horizons, shows the light.

So dare to tread where few have been,
To find the magic, deep within,
In unknown realms, our spirits find,
The hidden horizons of the mind.

Rewoven Journeys

Threads of gold in shadows spun,
A tapestry of life begun,
With every step and silent tear,
The journeys rewoven, become clear.

Memories stitched through time's cruel hand,
Yet in their weave, we understand,
A map unfolds, the past reveals,
The paths we took, our silent deals.

Each journey ends where one began,
The circle spins, each thread a plan,
In every heart, a story told,
Of rewoven journeys, brave and bold.

Through tangled knots and frayed desire,
We mended dreams, rewove the fire,
In every weft, a lesson learned,
Through rewoven journeys, hearts have turned.

So cherish threads of life's embrace,
Each journey etched in time and space,
For we are both, the warp and weft,
In rewoven journeys, none are left.

Inward Horizons

In silent moments, thoughts arise,
Within the soul, where whispers sing,
A journey vast, with endless skies,
Embracing all that life may bring.

Through valleys deep and hills so high,
Landscapes within, they come alive,
A traveler's heart, to never die,
Inward horizons, we survive.

The stars above, a mirrored glance,
Reflecting depths we dare not show,
In twilight's dance, we take our stance,
Discovering paths where shadows go.

Each step, a truth to be unveiled,
A secret wish to guide the way,
With every breath, the dreamers sailed,
Inward horizons, light of day.

The Crux of Me

In quiet hours of darkest night,
When silence holds the key to see,
A spark ignites a fleeting light,
Revealing depths, the crux of me.

Fragments of a soulful dream,
In whispered winds, they softly fly,
Unraveling what might have been,
In shadowed corners of the sky.

The essence lies beneath the veil,
A hidden truth, a sacred plea,
Through trials faced and triumph's tale,
Emerges whole, the crux of me.

In moments rare, the heart reveals,
The marrow of our deepest plea,
Each heartbeat true, the wound it heals,
Holding close the crux of me.

Beyond the Surface

Beneath the wave of daily strife,
Where currents flow in hidden streams,
Lies the essence of a life,
Far beyond our waking dreams.

In shadows cast by fleeting fears,
A deeper realm awaits to see,
Where silent whispers fill our ears,
Beyond the surface, there is me.

The echoes of a ancient song,
Resound within a vibrant heart,
In places where we all belong,
Beyond the surface, we're a part.

With eyes that seek the hidden hues,
And hearts that yearn for unity,
To paths unknown, we must pursue,
Beyond the surface, we are free.

Sculpting the Inner Truth

In marble veins and granite lines,
The sculptor's hands create anew,
From thought to form, in patient signs,
Emerges all that's pure and true.

Each chisel stroke, a quest to find,
The core that lies in frozen stone,
In every curve, the soul defined,
In every shape, the spirit shown.

With careful grace, the artist's touch,
Reveals what eyes alone can't see,
In silent calm, through hands so much,
The inner truth begins to be.

Through each creation, heart and mind,
Bring forth a world both bold and smooth,
In every piece, a truth refined,
Sculpting the depths of inner truth.

Touchstone of Memory

Beneath the ancient, whispering tree,
Memories like leaves unfurl,
Their stories dancing on the breeze,
Of a once familiar world.

Footsteps echo on silent streets,
Ghosts of laughter in the air,
Time suspended, moments meet,
In the tenderest of care.

Eyes closed tight, I conjure scenes,
Faces lost to history's shade,
In my heart, each moment gleams,
A bond that will not fade.

Past and present weave as one,
Threads of gold and silver spun,
In the twilight, under sun,
A tapestry begun.

In the sanctuary of the mind,
Reflections ripple like a stream,
In the touchstone I can find,
The essence of a dream.

Homeland of the Heart

In the cradle of earth and sky,
Where mountains rise and rivers flow,
Beneath the watchful eagle's eye,
A place where hearts will grow.

Whispers of the willow's song,
Echoes through the valley's hum,
In this land where dreams belong,
To the soil from which we're sprung.

Each path and trail familiar known,
By footsteps marking time's own art,
In every stone, a story sown,
This homeland of the heart.

Fields of gold and oceans blue,
In sunrise's gentle start,
To this place we all are true,
Homeland of the heart.

Even when from afar we roam,
Our souls remain apart,
Drawn back to this eternal home,
In the homeland of the heart.

Inner Sanctum

Deep within the soul's retreat,
Where shadows dance with light,
Silence reigns in calm defeat,
Against the endless night.

There the spirit finds its rest,
Amidst the worries, fear's parade,
In the caverns of the chest,
Stillness there is made.

Thoughts take flight on wings unseen,
To realms where dreams reside,
In this sacred space serene,
Found within the tide.

A haven from the stormy seas,
Where troubled waters calm,
In the whispered autumn breeze,
All is safe from harm.

Sanctuary deep inside,
A fortress of the mind,
Where peace and purpose yet abide,
In the inner sanctum find.

Voice From Within

From the quiet depths below,
A whisper breathes its way to light,
Guiding where the heart should go,
Through the shadows of the night.

In the silence of the soul,
A voice arises, pure and clear,
Calling us to make us whole,
Banish doubt, dispel the fear.

Through the din of daily life,
It speaks of truths we fail to see,
Amidst the chaos and the strife,
A path to tranquility.

Listen close, and you shall hear,
The wisdom of an age untold,
Born of love that conquers fear,
A beacon in the cold.

Heed the voice that whispers still,
From within the heart it calls,
Offering a guiding will,
Lifting spirits when they fall.

Full Circle's Embrace

In the twilight's gentle grace,
We begin our humble race.
From dawn to dusk, life's tender chase,
Completes in full circle's embrace.

Whispers of the memories past,
In the evening's shadows cast.
Hearts converge, their beats contrast,
Finding peace that ever lasts.

Waves that kiss the silent shore,
Echo tales of lives before.
With each tide we learn and more,
In the circle's core we soar.

Soul's Canvas

With a brush of thought, I paint,
Dreams that wander, never faint.
Colors blend without restraint,
On the soul's vast canvas, quaint.

In the hues of joy and sorrow,
Brighter dawns from dark tomorrow.
Every stroke, a tale we borrow,
Crafting realms where hearts may follow.

Through the shades of life's embrace,
Truths and secrets interlace.
On this canvas, pure in grace,
We behold our mirrored space.

Lingering Reflections

In the mirror of the mind,
Echoes of our thoughts confined.
Lingering reflections bind,
Stories lost and moments kind.

Shadows dance on memories fraught,
Lessons learned, and battles fought.
In each glimmer, wisdom's bought,
Reflections that our souls have sought.

Glimpses of our yesterdays,
Shimmer in the twilight haze.
In the silence, voices raise,
Lingering in time's own maze.

Chasing Inner Stars

Beneath the sky's vast tapestry,
Lie dreams that venture wild and free.
Chasing inner stars we see,
Lights that guide our destiny.

Through the dark and winding night,
Glimmers whisper, soft and bright.
We pursue the astral light,
Inward bound, our spirits' flight.

Every wish upon a star,
Maps the paths we've traveled far.
Guiding who we truly are,
In our hearts, a cosmic scar.

Emerging From Shadows

In the cloak of midnight's veil,
Whispers of the dawn prevail,
Stars retreat as skies unite,
Welcoming the morning light.

Shadows dance with soft embrace,
Fading in the sun's own grace,
Old fears scatter, new hopes near,
Light dispels what once was here.

Steps emerge from where they'd hide,
Paths anew with each new stride,
Courage mends what darkness tore,
Life begins to stretch and soar.

Echoes of the past might call,
But no longer can they stall,
For the heart now knows its way,
Guided by the break of day.

In that glow, the shadows end,
And the soul begins to mend,
Emerging whole, the spirit sighs,
Touched by light, the darkness flies.

Journey to Wholeness

Amidst the broken shards of time,
Lies the path to the sublime,
Winding through the heart's deep cracks,
Finding light where darkness lacks.

Puzzle pieces, once askew,
Form a picture clear and true,
With each step, the journey's song,
Mends what's shattered, makes it strong.

Threads of hope and strands of grace,
Weave a tapestry in place,
Stitch by stitch, the wounds transform,
In the calm, after the storm.

Eyes that once were blind to see,
Now reflect a unity,
In the journey, wholeness found,
Lost and searching, now unbound.

Through the trials, pain will cease,
Giving way to inner peace,
Journey's end, as hearts align,
Whole at last, in love divine.

Restoring the Portrait

Canvas marred by years gone by,
Brushstrokes fade, pigments dry,
Time distorts the image clear,
Yet the essence lingers near.

With each touch, a careful hand,
Paths of color, grains of sand,
Gently coaxing life anew,
From where the shadows once withdrew.

Layered history, unveiled,
Truth and beauty both regaled,
Every mark, a story told,
In the hues of bright and bold.

Memory and present blend,
Fragments join and fissures mend,
In the strokes, a love portrayed,
Line by line, the fears allayed.

Restoration of the soul,
In the art, both part and whole,
Portrait gleams with life restored,
Journey captured, hope adored.

The Underlying Loom

In the intricate design,
Threads of fate and dreams align,
Patterns hidden, yet they show,
In the weave, the truths we know.

Every strand and every hue,
Tells a tale both old and new,
Warp and weft in perfect blend,
Crafts a story without end.

Hidden whispers in the seams,
Echoes of forgotten dreams,
Yet the loom, with patient care,
Binds them with a thread so rare.

Cycles turning, threads unwind,
Secrets of the heart we find,
In the fabric of our days,
Woven paths and sacred ways.

Mysteries, they intertwine,
In each knot, a love divine,
Underlying loom reveals,
All the beauty the heart feels.

Paths Cross Again

Under the twilight's gentle glow,
We wander through the evening's flow.
Our journeys twined, our steps align,
In moments brief, our hearts design.

In whispers soft, past echoes play,
As memories hold nights at bay.
The past and present softly blend,
When paths once crossed, now meet again.

A glance, a smile, familiar eyes,
In silence shared, no need for lies.
Two souls rejoined in destiny's bind,
A fleeting touch, a fate unlined.

We walk as one, then part in grace,
The night's embrace, our sacred space.
Though time may drift in endless streams,
Paths cross again in timeless dreams.

Awakening the Spirit

In dawn's embrace, a fresh new start,
The world awakes, with tender heart.
The spirit stirs, from slumber deep,
To find the strength, from dreams we reap.

Through morning's light, the soul takes flight,
From shadows dark to realms of bright.
With every step, the fire ignites,
Awakening the spirit's might.

In every breath, in every stride,
The essence grows, nowhere to hide.
A journey vast, both tough and grand,
As spirit wakes, it takes its stand.

With eyes unclouded, heart so clear,
The spirit soars, beyond all fear.
For in awakening, we find
The boundless power of the mind.

Sanctuary of the Self

Amidst the noise, a haven found,
A silent place, where thoughts abound.
Within this space, the self seeks rest,
A sanctuary, we know best.

Beneath the stars, with moonlight's gleam,
In solitude, we start to dream.
The mind's retreat, a sheltered bay,
Where worries drift, and fade away.

Here lies the truth, in stillness kept,
The secrets guarded, the tears wept.
In silence deep, the self reveals,
The hidden wounds, the scars it heals.

This refuge built, with inner light,
A cherished shard of darkest night.
In sanctuary, soul finds peace,
Within ourselves, our own release.

Luminous Return

When shadows part, the light returns,
The heart, once dim, now brightly burns.
Through nights endured with silent cries,
The dawn emerges, no disguise.

A world reborn in golden hue,
The luminous return is true.
With every ray, a promise cast,
The pain of yore, now firmly past.

The day begins with newfound grace,
Illuminates each hidden trace.
In light we see, in light we grow,
The path ahead begins to show.

Embrace the glow, let shadows fall,
For in its warmth, we stand tall.
Our souls renewed, the journey clear,
The luminous return is here.

Back to Origins

In ancient fields where shadows dance,
I find my roots in whispered trance,
The soil beneath, a sacred stance,
Returns my heart to life's first glance.

With every step on paths of old,
The stories of the past unfold,
The echoes of the ancients told,
A lineage of hearts so bold.

I breathe the air that once they did,
Unveil the mysteries they hid,
A timeless bond that cannot rid,
The essence of where life begins.

To origins, my soul shall trace,
In nature's lap, a warm embrace,
A journey back to time and space,
Where first I saw the world's wide face.

United with the earth we tread,
In endless cycles, never dead,
The origins where love is fed,
A sacred path that lies ahead.

Labyrinth of the Soul

In winding mazes, deep and dark,
The soul embarks on quests to mark,
Its essence with the inner spark,
A labyrinth where dreams embark.

Around each bend, a lesson found,
In silence where the heart is bound,
A whisper of the soul's true sound,
In shadows where its truths are crowned.

Conflicting paths, the mind's own play,
Where light and dark both love to sway,
The soul emerges from the fray,
In wisdom gained from night and day.

Through corridors of joy and grief,
The soul finds light in each relief,
In every trial, every belief,
The journey of the heart's motif.

From labyrinthine thoughts unfurled,
A deeper truth is gently twirled,
The essence of a richer world,
Within the soul's sweet pearls unfurled.

Tracing My Steps

On paths once wandered, now I tread,
To trace the steps where dreams have led,
With every footprint, stories spread,
A journey through the life we've shed.

In every mark upon the ground,
The echoes of the past rebound,
In silent whispers, they resound,
A map of memories profound.

The steps I take, both small and grand,
Recount the tales of sea and land,
Each stride a link in life's own band,
A symphony, a guiding hand.

To find the places once held dear,
I follow footprints crystal clear,
In tracing steps, the past is near,
The soul's own path through time's frontier.

And as the journey reaches close,
The present meets the past that shows,
A tapestry of highs and lows,
In steps retraced where spirit grows.

Eternal Homecoming

The journey ends where it began,
In fields where dreams and memories ran,
To find the heart where love began,
The sacred space of home's own plan.

In every whisper of the trees,
The call of home is on the breeze,
A gentle song that soothes and frees,
The spirit found in earth and seas.

Returning to the hearth so warm,
Where love and life both take their form,
A refuge bosom to the storm,
In endless cycles, hearts transform.

Through wayward paths and distant lands,
We find the touch of tender hands,
A circle formed with golden bands,
Eternal love where home still stands.

In coming home, our souls align,
In spaces where the stars do shine,
A peace, a light, so pure, divine,
The homecoming that's truly thine.

Vindication of the Soul

In shadows deep, the spirit roams,
Through veils of night, seeking light,
With every step, a burden looms,
A flicker bright, in endless night.

Face darkened past, confront and see,
The wrongs, the rights, the silent plea,
Through trials borne, a soul set free,
In justice found, we cease to flea.

Redemption's voice, a call so clear,
Echoes in the heart, devoid of fear,
With truth as guide, the path sincere,
In vindication, we persevere.

Rise from depths, embrace the dawn,
With strength renewed, the chains are gone,
A soul repents, and battles on,
In sacred light, reborn anon.

With grace, the spirit finds its place,
In love's embrace, and endless space,
Through time, through pain, we seek the face,
Of peace, within, a pure embrace.

The Inner Sanctum

Inward gaze to a silent sea,
A realm within, where heartbeats flee,
Where whispers soft, and shadows be,
The core of self, the soul's decree.

Through woven dreams and secret rites,
In stillness found, no need for lights,
The quiet vast, where peace ignites,
Beyond the day's imposing sights.

Deep reflections, ripples spread,
In thought's pure stream, by wisdom led,
Through echoes of the words unsaid,
Resides the soul, well-anchored, fed.

A hidden world, serene and bright,
Where time stands still in endless night,
The inner sanctum, pure and right,
A sanctuary, out of sight.

Seek not the noise of life's demand,
But wander through this sacred land,
For here, within, you'll understand,
The truest self, and peace at hand.

Inward Bound

Beyond the veil of worldly calls,
Where silent streams of wisdom flow,
To inner depths where truth enthralls,
In quiet waves, the soul to know.

Through labyrinths of thought and dream,
In shadows cast by distant gleam,
We venture forth, an inward scheme,
To find the heart's unspoken theme.

In whispering winds and gentle sighs,
The echoes of our past arise,
By introspective, yearning eyes,
We pierce the dark, unveil the skies.

Each step within, a journey long,
Where strength of spirit proves so strong,
Through doubt, resolve, we move along,
To harmonize our inner song.

With every breath, the calm is found,
In sacred space, on hallowed ground,
We chart the course of soul profound,
Inward bound, where truths abound.

Return to Clarity

Through mists of doubt, we seek the light,
In tangled thoughts, a guiding star,
To break the chains of endless night,
And find the truth of who we are.

In chaos wild, the mind does roam,
Lost in shadows, far from home,
Yet in the heart, a steady tome,
An anchor deep, no need to roam.

With every tear, a vision clears,
Through trials faced and silent fears,
A path revealed, through countless years,
To wisdom's shores, our conscience steers.

The fog dissolves, the way is bright,
Each step, a beacon, pure delight,
With open eyes, embrace the sight,
In clarity, our hearts unite.

Return to self, in peace, we stand,
With open hearts and outstretched hand,
In every breath, a truth so grand,
In clarity, we understand.

The Inner Pilgrimage

Through sunsets and twilight's whispered glow,
Journeys within, where shadows know,
Paths obscure, yet hearts imbue,
Ancient secrets, ever true.

In silence deep, the soul embarks,
Tracing dreams of fleeting sparks,
Echoes of wisdom, softly sung,
Guiding where the spirit sprung.

Rivers of thought in reverie,
Flowing toward the inner sea,
Currents of love, waves of peace,
From earthly bounds a sweet release.

Mountains within, vast and grand,
Climbs of faith our feet withstand,
Breath of life in quiet lands,
Touching places no eye scans.

Circle complete, vision clear,
Truth revealed, ever near,
Journey inward, bound in grace,
Finding home within each face.

Soul's Refuge

In realms where shadows fail to tread,
Soul's refuge from the stormy dread,
Sanctuary for heart and mind,
In inner peace, a haven find.

Echoes fade of worldly din,
In silent spaces, peace begins,
A warm embrace in twilight's glow,
In solitude the spirit grows.

Gardens of the quiet heart,
Where worries pierce, but leave no scar,
Verdant fields of thought and dream,
Soothing balm, a gentle stream.

Eyes turned inward, there reside,
Shelters where our fears subside,
In stillness, we are made anew,
Finding strength to see us through.

Soul's refuge ever near,
Soft and calm, dispelling fear,
In sanctuary of the mind,
Solace for all humankind.

Dawn of Rediscovery

In morning light, the shadows part,
Journey's dawn, a hopeful start,
Whispers of dreams once lost,
Healing from the night's cold frost.

With every step on fresh terrain,
Old wounds mend, release the pain,
Eyes alight with newfound sight,
Embrace the day, ignite the light.

Murmurs of forgotten lore,
Awakened hearts to seek once more,
Paths of yore now brightly shine,
Reclaimed wonder intertwined.

As petals bloom in early sun,
Miracles in life begun,
With open hearts, minds expand,
We touch the spark with gentle hands.

Dawn of rediscovery,
Wandering souls feel truly free,
In sunrise glow, find and see,
Treasures of our destiny.

Journey to the Heart

Across the realms of thought and time,
Mystery's pulse, a silent rhyme,
Voyage to the heart within,
Revealing truths where dreams begin.

With each step, the veil is thin,
Boundaries break, allowing in,
Shades of love and hues of grace,
Drawing near to the heart's embrace.

Paths entwine in subtle ways,
Guiding through life's tangled maze,
A compass held in inner light,
Navigates through darkest night.

In the heart, all answers lie,
Where reason ends and feelings fly,
An epic quest of boundless worth,
Rooted deep in sacred earth.

Journey deep, the essence find,
Unity of heart and mind,
In the chambers pure and vast,
The final truth revealed at last.

Renewal of Essence

In the quiet dawn, I find my peace,
Where shadows part and sorrows cease.
Renewal's breath upon the air,
A promise whispered, soft yet fair.

The river's edge, a tranquil stream,
Reflects my soul's rekindled dream.
Each day anew, the essence flows,
Through verdant fields where freedom grows.

The sun's embrace, a warm caress,
Dispels the night, removes distress.
In nature's lap, I lay my head,
With leaves and wind, my fears are shed.

The essence pure, beyond the guise,
Reveals the truth, dispels the lies.
In every dawn, a chance to see,
The boundless love that sets me free.

Time's Soft Whisper

A whisper soft, like morning's dew,
Through time's embrace, our paths renew.
In shadows cast by fleeting light,
We chase our dreams, both day and night.

The gentle tick of time's embrace,
Draws lines unseen upon our face.
Yet in its course, we find our way,
Through silent nights and golden days.

Moments pass like falling leaves,
A tapestry of life it weaves.
In whispers soft, the secrets hide,
Of journeys past and tears we've cried.

Eternal dance, the clock's refrain,
With every tick, both joy and pain.
In time's soft whisper, hearts align,
A fleeting glance, a love divine.

Restoration of My Core

Beneath the stars, my spirit mends,
Where broken dreams and hope transcends.
In quiet nights, I find my truth,
The ancient path that heals my youth.

With every step, the burdens fade,
In moonlight's glow, my fears allayed.
A sacred space within the heart,
Begins anew, a fresh restart.

In whispered winds, old wounds are healed,
Through nature's touch, my soul is steeled.
A journey back to what I knew,
Restoration, pure and true.

From deep within, a light is found,
A faithful guide, without a sound.
To mend the core and rise once more,
A spirit free, forever soar.

The Pathway Inward

Through silent woods, my journey lies,
A pathway inward, no disguise.
With every step, the world grows still,
And I embrace my inner will.

The trees around, a verdant hall,
In whispers speak, both large and small.
They guard the secrets, old and wise,
Revealing truths to opened eyes.

In each footfall, a story told,
Of ancient lands and hearts of gold.
The inward path, a sacred quest,
Where mind and soul find perfect rest.

Through shadows deep and lightway bright,
I seek the dawn, the inner light.
A pilgrimage to find my core,
Where peace resides forevermore.

The Veiled Return

A whisper in the twilight's glow,
Soft footsteps on forgotten trails,
The wind carries secrets lost in time,
Unraveling the ancient tales.

Mist drapes the forest in silver lace,
Moonlight pierces through shaded dreams,
Echoes of the past resurge,
In the haunting of shadowed gleams.

The stars bear witness to the rite,
Of returns from the shrouded past,
A figure cloaked in memories,
Walking through the night at last.

Eyes like embers, burning bright,
A journey veiled in mystery,
The heart yearns for the familiar,
In the dance of history.

With every step, the ghostly fade,
Blurs the line of present, past,
In the veiled return, a new beginning,
Emerges from the shadows cast.

Hidden Symphony

In the hush of dawn's embrace,
Notes unseen begin to rise,
A symphony of nature's grace,
Unfolds beneath the skies.

Whispers of the quiet leaves,
Dance upon the morning air,
Melodies the heart believes,
Are secret, pure, and rare.

The river hums a tender tune,
As it winds through meadow green,
Crickets join with stars and moon,
In a song calm and serene.

Voices of a hidden choir,
Blend in harmony so sweet,
Invisible, yet inspiring,
Every soul they meet.

In this hidden symphony,
Lies the magic of the land,
A reminder of what we cannot see,
Shared by nature, hand in hand.

The Unseen Journey

Beyond the horizon, a path unfurls,
In shadows of twilight's gentle hand,
An unseen journey, free and wild,
Traverses the uncharted land.

Footsteps silent, trail unknown,
Marked by whispers of the breeze,
Through valleys deep, over peaks of stone,
Guided by the ancient trees.

The soul wanders where few have dared,
Eyes closed, heart open wide,
Seeking truths, the world has spared,
In the space where dreams confide.

Stars align, a compass bright,
Leading through the endless night,
Each step, a story left to write,
In the tapestry of light.

In the end, the unseen journey's grace,
Reveals a world, stark and new,
A testament to the endless chase,
For the path concealed from view.

Silent Reclamation

In the quiet fields of dawn,
Where shadows yield to morning light,
A silent reclamation draws,
Reviving dreams once lost to night.

Soft winds whisper through the grass,
Echoes of the past return,
Silent vows in the shadows cast,
Await the dawn, patient and stern.

Nature's hand reclaims her own,
With gentle strength, with timeless grace,
In the silent space where seeds are sown,
She reweaves the empty place.

Ruins cloaked in verdant green,
Silent witnesses to time,
Reclaimed by life, unseen,
In a dance both pure and prime.

In the stillness, hearts renew,
Finding peace in reclaimed lands,
A silent reclamation true,
Crafted by unseen hands.

Memory of Me

In shadows cast, my thoughts entwine,
A dance of light, a trace defined,
Whispered echoes from moments past,
In memory's mirror, shadows last.

Fleeting glimpses, fragments clear,
Faces soften, voices near,
Through the fog, a smile remains,
A timeless thread in memory's chains.

Bound by whispers, soft and low,
Forgotten laughter starts to glow,
In corners where the silence meets,
A heart retraces bygone beats.

Yet in the dim, the essence stays,
A gentle touch through endless days,
For though time flees so swiftly past,
In memory's warmth, I hold fast.

Restoration of Spirit

In quiet peace, the spirit mends,
Where nature's hymn with hope blends,
A soothing balm, the world bestows,
In silent strength, calm rivers flow.

Through fields of gold, where breezes sing,
And birds on hopeful branches cling,
The heart finds rhythm, gentle, pure,
A deeper bond that shall endure.

In moments still, the soul revives,
With whispered winds, the spirit thrives,
A newfound purpose, bold and bright,
Emerging from the depths of night.

With every dawn, the spirit soars,
Through open skies and boundless shores,
Restored within, distinct and clear,
With courage vast and vision dear.

Veil of Time Lifted

When time's thin veil begins to rise,
Through hidden truths and unveiled skies,
A world awaits with eyes anew,
In moments grasped, in morning's hue.

What once obscured by past's embrace,
Now crystal clear in present's grace,
Each breath a gift, each step a song,
The path ahead, both wide and long.

In life's grand quilt, each thread revealed,
A story sewn, with wounds healed,
No more the shroud of yesterday,
A future bright in vast array.

With heart unbound, the spirit glows,
Through trials faced, true wisdom grows,
For in the lifting, we shall find,
The timeless bonds of heart and mind.

Uncharted Frontiers Within

In silent depths, where shadows play,
Unseen horizons softly sway,
An inward voyage just begins,
To uncharted frontiers within.

Through maze of thoughts, through layers deep,
Where secrets whispered, long to keep,
A journey vast, the soul embarks,
To inner realms where mystery sparks.

Each step reveals a hidden light,
In corners dark, new visions bright,
A world unknown beneath the skin,
The vast expanse of worlds within.

With open heart and courage strong,
To pathways new where souls belong,
Exploring realms with fearless stride,
Uncharted frontiers now untied.

Tracing the Roots

In ancient woods where echoes rest,
Whispers dance with leaves at best,
Mossy trails where footsteps tread,
   Histories in greens and red.

From roots that reach the earth's deep core,
   Stories rise of days of yore,
Tales untold in bark and branch,
Echoes from the forest's ranch.

Downward dig the ancient trees,
Veins of life beneath the breeze,
   Every ring a chapter spun,
Wars and peace, all battles won.

Silent voices of the past,
In wood and root, forever cast,
Through verdant paths, we trace our line,
To origins where earth aligns.

With every step, a journey back,
To whispered winds on nature's track,
In tracing roots, we find our guide,
A heritage where truths reside.

The Mirror Revisited

In silvered glass, reflections play,
Echoes of a bygone day,
Faces past and visions new,
Survey the world and bid adieu.

Each visage tells a story clear,
Of love and loss, of joy and fear,
Captured in a frame of light,
Mirrors hold our inner sight.

The glass, a portal to the soul,
Through which our hidden secrets stroll,
Moments frozen, time stood still,
In mirrored depths, our hearts refill.

With every glance, a memory stirs,
The past, the future, all occurs,
Reflections weave a tapestry,
Of who we are and dare to be.

Returning to the glass once more,
To see who we've become, explore,
In the mirror's gaze, we find,
The journey of our heart and mind.

Convergence of Being

In the silence where all thoughts blend,
Where self and universe contend,
A place where time and space converge,
Minds and spirits dare to merge.

Across the void, connections weave,
Threads of being none perceive,
A tapestry of life and dream,
In cosmic flow, we find the seam.

Energies of hearts align,
In realms where human souls entwine,
The dance of stars and mortal breath,
A unity surpassing death.

Here, all moments coexist,
In the continuum's gentle twist,
An endless cycle, birth and fade,
In the essence, all is made.

At that point where being meets,
Harmony in endless beats,
The convergence, all-enfolding,
In that space, the truth is holding.

Cradle of Essence

In the heart of night and day,
Where reality starts to sway,
Lies a cradle soft and deep,
Where our dreams and spirits sleep.

Cradle of the essence pure,
In its hold, all doubts obscure,
Nurtured in a tender space,
Guided by a gentle grace.

Stars above and earth below,
In this nest, emotions grow,
Roots of thought and branches spread,
Life's potential gently fed.

In this haven, time is still,
Echoes form and hearts fulfill,
Each breath taken, life anew,
Cradled essence, bright and true.

From this place, we rise again,
Wiser, stronger, free of pain,
For in the essence, held so near,
Lies the power to persevere.

Unveiling the Mask

Beneath the surface, hidden frames
An enigmatic dance of flames
In shadows deep, our secrets bask
The heart reveals, unveiling the mask

Fragmented truths in whispers lie
A silken thread in twilight sky
Concealed in art, emotions vast
The soul uncovers, unveiling the mask

A mirrored face in pale moon's light
Reflects a tale veiled in the night
Emerging bold, forsaking past
With courage clear, unveiling the mask

In fragile hands, the veil is torn
From shadows dim, new worlds are born
The silent echoes, questions ask
The mind transcends, unveiling the mask

An inner peace as storms abate
A dawn reborn, divine and great
In truth discovered, dreams unmask
The heart now free, unveiling the mask

The Silent Pilgrimage

A journey starts with silent tread
A path unseen, by heart is led
Through night's embrace and dawn's new page
We walk alone, the silent pilgrimage

With every step, a story told
Of dreams once lost, of hearts consoled
In tranquil woods or mountain's edge
We find our truth, the silent pilgrimage

An inward quest for peace and grace
In solitude, the soul's embrace
No bells to ring, no words to pledge
In sacred calm, the silent pilgrimage

The winding road, through night and day
In silent reverie, souls pray
The universe, our minds engage
Upon this path, the silent pilgrimage

With open heart and steady stride
Through unseen realms, we softly glide
In silence found, our souls engage
We find our home, the silent pilgrimage

Soul's Resurrection

From ashes cold, a spark ignites
A phoenix rises in twilight
In shadows deep, where sorrows reign
The soul reborn, sheds past's deep stain

The chains of yore, now cracked and fall
In silence heard, a distant call
With wings anew, and heart aflame
The soul ascends, free of its shame

In luminous night's tender embrace
Through trials faced, a certain grace
Emerging strong where shadows weep
The soul's revival, from dark and deep

Through ancient scars and whispered pain
A dawn arises, breaks the chain
With each new breath, a promise kept
The soul awakens from its sleep

Resilient light in darkest night
A spirit soaring towards the light
Renewed with hope, and firm protection
The journey starts, the soul's resurrection

www.ingramcontent.com/pod-product-compliance
Lightning Source LLC
LaVergne TN
LVHW020451070526
838199LV00063B/4909